10 95

THE SIRENS

MONSTERS OF MYTHOLOGY

25 VOLUMES

Hellenic

Amycus
Anteus
The Calydonian Boar
Cerberus
Chimaera
The Cyclopes
The Dragon of Boeotia
The Furies
Geryon
Harpalyce
Hecate
The Hydra
Ladon
Medusa
The Minotaur
The Nemean Lion
Procrustes
Scylla and Charybdis
The Sirens
The Spear-birds
The Sphinx

Norse

Fafnir
Fenris

Celtic

Drabne of Dole
Pig's Ploughman

MONSTERS OF MYTHOLOGY

THE SIRENS

Bernard Evslin

CHELSEA HOUSE PUBLISHERS

New York   New Haven   Philadelphia

1988

EDITOR
Jennifer Caldwell

ART DIRECTOR
Giannella Garrett

PICTURE RESEARCHER
Susan Quist

DESIGNER
Victoria Tomaselli

CREATIVE DIRECTOR
Harold Steinberg

First Printing

1 3 5 7 9 8 6 4 2

Library of Congress Cataloging-in-Publication Data

Evslin, Bernard.
The Sirens.

(Monsters of mythology)
Summary: Describes the origins of the sirens,
half-women, half-birds, who lured sailors
to their deaths with their irresistible voices,
and relates their encounter with Ulysses.
1. Sirens (Mythology)—Juvenile literature.
[1. Sirens (Mythology) 2. Mythology, Greek]
I. Title. II. Series: Evslin, Bernard. Monsters
of mythology.
BL820.S5E95   1988   398.2′1′0938   87-14602

ISBN 1-55546-258-8

Printed in Singapore

The goddess Athena promised a tiny
fishing village that it would become
the most famous city in the world if
it took her name. And, as a sign of
her pledge, she planted a wonderful tree.
Thousands of years later, a little girl
took the name of this tree as her own.
It is to her, my granddaughter, Olivia,
that I dedicate this book, which she will
read in time to come.

Characters

Monsters

The Sirens (SY rehnz)	A pair of winged sea nymphs, Teles (TELL uhs) and Ligiea (LY gee uh), whose voices call sailors to drown
The Jellyfish	A clot of the primal slime that feeds upon everything within reach

Gods

Zeus (ZOOS)	King of the Gods
Poseidon (poh SY duhn)	God of the Sea
Athena (uh THEE nuh)	Goddess of Wisdom
Hermes (HUR meez)	The Messenger God

Apollo (uh PAHL oh)	The Sun God
Artemis (AHR tuh mihs)	Goddess of the Moon
Ares (AIR eez)	God of War
Demeter (duh MEE tuhr)	Goddess of the Harvest
Hestia (HEHS tih uh)	Goddess of the Hearth
Aphrodite (af ruh DY tee)	Goddess of Love
Helios (HEE lih ohs)	A Titan who drove Apollo's sun chariot across the sky

Demigods

Circe (SUR see)	Daughter of the sun's charioteer; a highly skilled sorceress
Proteus (PROH tee uhs)	A changeable demigod who serves, and betrays, Poseidon
Cora (KOH ruh)	A meadow nymph

Mortals

Butes (BU teez)	A brave youth
Ulysses (u LIHS eez)	The greatest captain of antiquity—and since

Contents

1

The Owl Goddess

A n ancient proverb says:

When gods are at odds,
they bloody the sky,
and rivers run dry.
Monsters slay,
mortals die.

Indeed, the strange tale of the Sirens and their victims is rooted in the feud that raged between Athena, Goddess of Wisdom, and Poseidon, God of the Sea.

In the beginning, everything was alive. The earth twitched like a sleeping bear. The sea threw vast tantrums called tidal waves. Trees capered, rocks sang.

"This must cease," said Zeus to his High Council. "We gods can float serenely above such disorder. But the race of humans we have planted upon earth is a more fragile breed—unable to abide amid rollicking seas and frolicking trees and mountains that skip like rams. We shall have to impose a little order."

Thereupon, with one gesture Zeus froze the revels. Rocks fell silent; trees stopped dancing.

But there were creatures who inhabited the wild secret places; there were the nymphs of river and sea, of mountain, wood, and field; there were the goat-haunched satyrs of the grove, strong as stags, but so lightfooted no blade of grass bent under their hooves. These creatures, the naiads, dryads, and oreads, these musky antic satyrs, refused to obey the edict. Gathering all the vital mischief of the locked tides, the silenced rocks, and rooted trees, they roamed sea and earth trying to break the great taboo and recall everything to life, trying to kindle the untried hearts of those called human with a spark of the old green fire.

The naiads, dryads, and satyrs . . .
roamed sea and earth trying to break
the great taboo and recall everything to life.

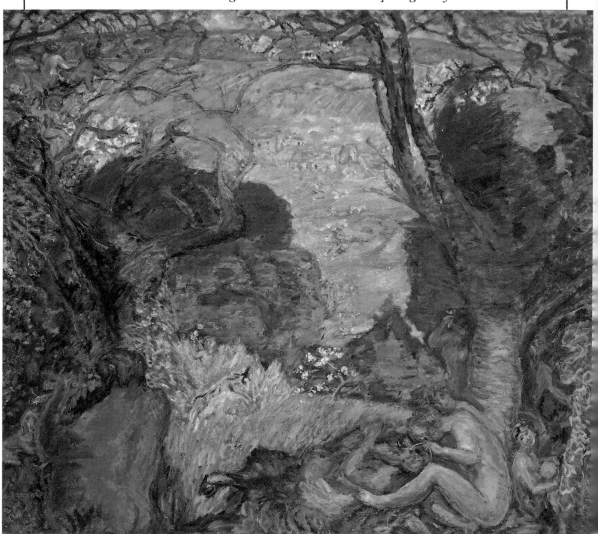

This thwarted wildness festered also in the hearts of the gods, who sought to amuse themselves by fighting with one another. Their feuds, that flared like summer lightning, blasted the total harmony designed by Zeus and shattered his enormous repose. He again summoned the gods to his throne room and imposed a second truce, promising eternal punishment to anyone violating its terms.

Now it was that a demigod named Proteus received a message from Athena, asking him to visit her. This Proteus happened to be a strangely talented creature who could change his shape in the twinkling of an eye and become any living thing he wished. He was also Poseidon's most trusted servant, and general tutor to the beautiful, sleek nereids who swarmed the Ocean Stream. Proteus was very surprised by this invitation from the owl goddess, for Athena was Poseidon's sworn enemy. But curiosity was stronger than doubt, and he hastened to her.

The place the goddess had chosen as her own was a certain mountain of the Olympian range. There she had set up a gigantic loom and spindle. Enthroned on her mountain, plucking cloud-wool and dyeing it in the lights of sunrise and sunset, she wove marvelous tapestries which she flung in colored scrolls across the sky.

Nearby loomed a strange rock formation—a cup-shaped boulder and, propped within it, a stone shaft, knobbed at one end. Together they resembled pestle and mortar, but enormous ones.

Although his curiosity was aflame, Proteus approached hesitantly. He was a bit afraid of the goddess. In all his changes he preferred small, meek females, and Athena was very tall, and anything but meek. For the hard climb he had transformed himself into a mountain goat, but just before reaching the top he resumed his favorite shape as a white seal.

"You are a welcome sight," said Athena, "although a strange one. It is not often that a seal is found at these altitudes."

"Not a bad choice, my lady. A fur coat is useful up here. The wind blows chill."

"Do you have any idea why I have sent for you?"

"None . . . but I am honored by the summons."

"As you may know, Zeus has declared a truce, prohibiting us gods from feuding with one another. And those of us who have no desire for peace shall have to find others to carry on our vendettas. My own plans for pursuing my quarrel with Poseidon are quite extensive, and I need your help."

"You wish me to betray my master?"

"Precisely," answered Athena. "Are you bribable?"

"In matters of morality we lesser breeds model ourselves upon the gods."

"Then you *are* bribable," declared Athena.

"What do you offer me to betray my master?"

"I am not so rich as Poseidon, you know, who commands the vast bounty of the sea. Nor as rich as Hades in whose inlaid ceiling of sky diamonds imitate stars, and whose floor of earth is veined with gold and silver. Basically, O Proteus, I have only wisdom to offer."

"I see."

"I know it doesn't sound like much compared to what is held in the coffers of earth and sea. But remember this; wisdom is the key that unlocks the secrets of nature. He who possesses only one of these secrets can enrich himself beyond the dreams of avarice."

"You don't know how avariciously I dream, O goddess."

"Beware, Proteus, I am not one to forget a favor refused. I don't ask that many, nor am I refused that often. And, in all modesty, I make a dangerous enemy."

"Please, Athena. Your threats frighten me so that I shall have to go to Poseidon with my tale. And he, in turn, will report to Zeus that you are planning to break the peace."

Her pale eyes were upon him. They were the color of the northern sea as it turns to ice. Proteus felt himself shudder. Seal-skin is extremely tough, and very densely furred, with a layer of blubber beneath it to give seals perfect protection against the arctic blasts. Nevertheless, those eyes stabbed through him like twin icicles, freezing him to the marrow. He found himself wondering how he had been able to muster courage to refuse this goddess anything.

Finally, her face broke into a smile. A wintry smile, to be sure, but better than the frown she had been wearing.

"Well," said Athena. "As dispenser of wisdom, I should be wise enough myself to know when a craving must go unsatisfied. I bear you no grudge, Proteus. And you must try not to think so unkindly of me."

"O goddess," cried Proteus, "I am overwhelmed by your forebearance, and truly regret my inability to help you. Permit me, by way of apology, to offer you this pearl I produced during my recent stint as an oyster. It is a flawless gem, as you can see—although, I must admit, your own beauty must dim the luster of any jewel."

"You are courteous and sweet-spoken, Proteus. Is there anything I can do for you before you leave?"

"I am very changeable," said Proteus. "I have so many selves that I don't know which is the real me."

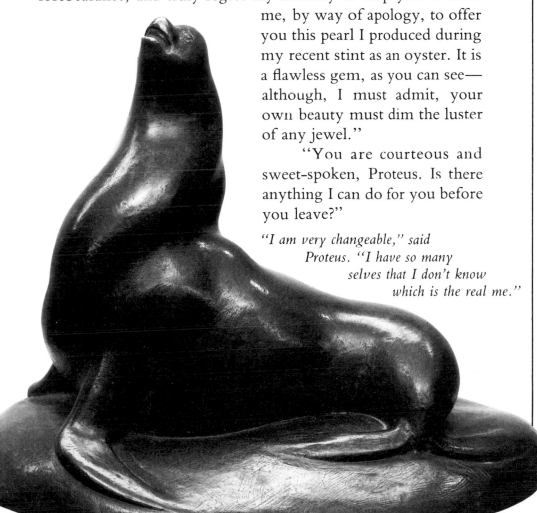

"Tell me, what is wisdom exactly?"

"Ah, my friend, it is too vast an attribute to be described in one sentence. I'll tell you this though: its central idea is 'know thyself.' "

"Is that better than knowing *yourself*?"

"Same thing, but in god-speak. More impressive."

"You see, goddess, I am very changeable. I have so many selves that I don't know which is the real me."

"The real you, eh? Shall I help you find it?" asked Athena.

"Can you?"

"We can try—together. Why don't you run through your changes for me?"

"Here? Now?"

"*Here* and *now* are two of my favorite words, Proteus. I have steeped them in wisdom."

"Do you want to see *all* my transformations? There are so many."

"First, answer a question for me out of your own special knowledge. Is it true that every enchantment bears within it its own thwart?"

"If by that, my lady, you mean a counter-spell, one that nullifies or reverses the magic, the answer is yes. But I've never tested the theory personally."

"Has no one ever tried to thwart your transformations?"

"They have. They have. But they have failed. From the first, I knew that whoever could seize me and hold me through three metamorphoses would prevent a fourth change and return me to the shape I first adopted."

"And no one has been able to do this?" asked Athena.

"No one," said Proteus. "You must understand that I can change myself into a wolf or crocodile, and snap off any hand that grasps me. Or become a viper, for example, and sting my captor to death."

"I see. . . . I see. Very interesting," said Athena. "Now,

why don't you show me a few of your favorite transformations, where the real you may perhaps reside. I know! Become once again the creature you were born."

"That is by no means my favorite incarnation," said Proteus. "In fact, it doesn't please me at all."

"Nevertheless," said Athena, "as I think of it, I do want you to begin there. I believe it will give us a clue to what we seek."

Proteus was thinking very fast. There was something about the situation that was making him uneasy. He never transformed himself idly, but only in response to some specific task, or some emergency. And the more he thought about it the less inclined he was to go through a series of changes under the gaze of this stern goddess who seemed to be growing taller every moment. Her shoulders and arms gleamed like marble now in the gathering dusk. And the icy stilettos of her eyes were skewering him, paralyzing his will.

He tried to fight free of her gaze, to simply bid her farewell, and depart. He heard her say, "Well, I'm waiting."

Still, he hesitated.

The goddess spoke again. Her words seemed to be falling from a great height. "Proteus, begin!" It was no longer a request; it was a command. He was unable to disobey. Hating himself, he returned to the shape he had worn when entering the world.

"What do you call this thing you're now being?" asked Athena. "I've never seen anything like it before."

"Sea-blob," he muttered.

"You look something like Phorcys, but even uglier, if possible. And smaller."

"Yes, I'm sort of a cousin to the Sea-hog."

"Very odd . . . let me look at you."

Her long arm reached out; she scooped him up and held him to her face. To his horror Proteus felt hands stronger than any he had ever felt before tightening about him.

Immediately, he changed himself into an eel and began to wriggle out of her clutch. But her strong fingers shifted, found a new grip, and squeezed tighter.

He became a bull in her grasp. His massive weight forced her arm down. He crashed to the ground, landing on his hooves, and whirled to gore her with his horns. But she had fallen with him, still clutching as she fell. Her grip grew tighter and tighter; she was under him. He rose into the air, trying to somersault and come down horns first, impaling her.

They were wrestling beside the giant loom. Still gripping him, Athena reached with her other hand and snatched a skein of thread. Moving with the weird celerity of a spider, she wrapped

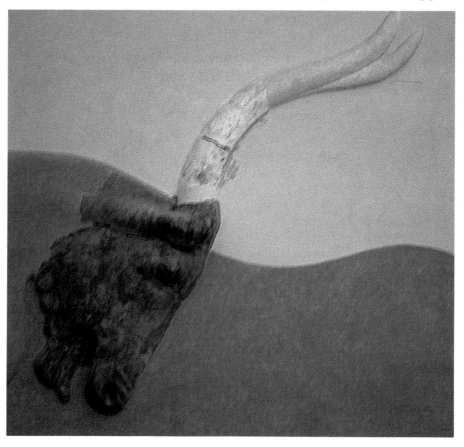

Proteus became a bull. . . . He crashed to the ground and whirled to gore Athena with his horns.

*Proteus changed into a tiger. . . .
Blazing with hatred, he
sprang full at Athena.*

him around and around. Now, this thread was not spun from cloud-wool or sheep's wool or earthly flax, but had been given to Athena in another story by Atropos, Destiny's Hag, who with her crone sisters spun the thread of life, measured it out, then stretched it or cut it. And this unique thread was fatal to freedom, and could bind anything in the world, however strong.

The bull lay trussed, helpless. Proteus changed into a tiger and slipped his bonds. Blazing with hatred, he sprang full at Athena, wanting to sink his claws into that snowy flesh and rip her to bloody rags.

She caught him in mid-leap and held him away from her body so that his claws could not reach her. He curled up, meaning to rake her with his hind claws, and tear her guts out. But all this time her arctic grey eyes were stabbing into the pools of green flame that were his eyes. Again, their ice entered him, cooling his tigerish blood, freezing his will. He tried to strike with his back claws but she held him off. She sat upon her throne, drawing him onto her lap. Her fingers were rods of power, sinking into his pelt, welding themselves to him. Her other hand stroked his fur.

All his rage dissolved. He felt a delicious languor filling him. He was a pussy-cat in the lap of a goddess. She had held

9

*He felt his tiger bones shrinking. . . . And he
was again what he had been born—a Sea-blob.*

him through three transformations. He felt his tiger bones shrinking, and his gorgeous hide turning into aspic. And he was again
what he had been born—a Sea-blob, magic thwarted, helpless in
her hands.

Proteus felt her turning his head so that he had to gaze upon the great stone pestle and mortar. "See that?" she asked.

"Yes, goddess."

"Know what I use it for?"

"No, goddess."

"I heap flowers in it and crush them to make the dyes that color my stuffs. Not only flowers—sometimes I crush other things."

"What other things?"

"Those that need crushing. *Now* do you understand why I wanted you to become a Sea-blob?"

"I hope not."

"In your present form you will fit very comfortably into that mortar, and should prove eminently crushable. I shall pound you into a jelly and boil that jelly into a potion. Use of that potion together with certain magic spells should enable me or anyone I designate to transform others into what shapes we will, giving us a distinct advantage over our enemies."

"Please, Athena! Don't pound me into a jelly. Don't boil me into a potion. I can be more useful to you, alive and intact."

"What, *you* !—who refuse me a small favor?"

"I am yours, body and soul!" cried Proteus. "Yours in all my variety; yours, flesh, bone, marrow, and wit. The cold blades of your eyes have cut my own will out of me as a fishwife fillets a flounder. I am yours, entirely yours. Command, and I perform."

"I don't know, Proteus."

"At least let me try. What are you risking? You can always catch me again and put me into your mortar."

"Very well, you have convinced me."

"Thank you, thank you."

"Now listen carefully," said Athena. "I have recruited a very promising young witch called Circe. Are you acquainted with her?"

Across the entire Middle Sea basin,
Poseidon was the god
most fervently worshiped.

"The sun god Helios has a daughter by that name," said Proteus. "Very tall, flame-haired, willful, a dangerous beauty, in fact."

"That's the one," said Athena. "She is to be my chief agent in the struggle against Poseidon. I want you to go to the Isle of Sobs where Circe dwells and instruct her in the techniques of transformation."

"I shall do so, goddess."

"To accomplish her task, however, she will need two assistants, whom you will furnish. You must search the Ocean Stream for a pair of the strongest, swiftest, cleverest sea nymphs you can find. You will bring them along with you to the Isle of Sobs and train them to assist Circe in her performance of the dark arts."

"Very well, goddess."

"Are you sure you understand what I require?" asked Athena. "Any error or omission on your part I shall view as simple disobedience, and shall punish severely."

"As I understand it," said Proteus, "I am to train Circe in the art of transformation. Find two sea nymphs and train them as well."

"Correct," said Athena. "Succeed, and prosper. Fail, and suffer."

Athena was happy with the plot she was weaving. She planned to attack Poscidon at his most prideful point and turn his strength to weakness. For the sea god, like all gods, was nourished by worship. He spread terror upon the waters until those who traveled the sea, or farmed its waters or dwelt by its shores, had been taught to beg for mercy. Before embarking on a voyage, sailors would sacrifice to him, and pray for fair winds. Fishermen would pray for a rich harvest of fish, pirates, for plunder. And those who dwelt on the coast would beseech him to withhold his

What Athena planned was to set Circe and her nymphs astride the busiest sea-lane.

storms, or at least, strike some-where else. Across the entire Middle Sea basin, Poseidon was the god most fervently worshiped.

What Athena now planned was to set Circe and her nymphs astride the busiest sea-lane and have them wreck ships and en-slave their crews. Whereupon, the goddess reasoned, seamen, finding their prayers unan-swered, would withdraw their faith in Poseidon and sacrifice upon other altars. Thus, Athena would be making her enemy suf-fer in the only way that gods can suffer—by being diminished.

As we know, Proteus had been thoroughly terrified by Athena; he was now obeying every one of her instructions. He combed the sea for the two strongest, swiftest, cleverest nereids. In the waters off the sic-kle-shaped island called Corfu, he found a pair of sisters named Teles and Ligiea. He invited them to the Isle of Sobs to assist

Proteus combed the sea
for the two strongest,
swiftest, cleverest nereids.

14

Circe in her sorceries. At first, they refused. They relished the boisterous, free life of the ocean. They loved to follow fishing boats, capsize them, and swim off with the handsomest lads.

As it happened, though, the fisher-folk had grown cautious of late; their boats hugged the shore, and the sea nymphs had been hunting in vain. When Proteus told them that Circe practiced a magic that could trap the wiliest crews, the nereids dropped their objections and agreed to join the sorceress on the Isle of Sobs.

2

The Isle of Sobs

or the first month or so, all went well as Proteus taught Circe and the two nercids the arts of transformation. Circe was a natural sorceress, already adept at the basic spells and incantations, and she learned faster than Proteus could teach. The nymphs, although not so talented as Circe, were fascinated by magic, and very eager for instruction. Nevertheless, after a while, Proteus found himself growing quietly frantic.

Although things seemed peaceable, he sensed a feud simmering between Circe and the nymphs. He knew that if the quarrel flared into open warfare, it would disrupt Athena's plans, and he would be held responsible. The goddess, enraged, might very well pluck him off the island and pop him into her great stone mortar, pound him to a pulp with her stone pestle, then boil him into a potion. So he was desperate to patch up a truce.

He knew that it was Circe who was mostly to blame in this matter. She was very proud, and fiendishly jealous—qualities which often go together. Although only a demigoddess, she considered herself as regal and potent as anyone in the Pantheon, and entitled to the same divine honors. This opinion was not shared by the nereids, who hadn't a reverential bone in their supple

Circe was very proud, and fiendishly jealous.

bodies. They viewed her not as a goddess, but as an arrogant redheaded witch, full of insufferable pretensions.

The more Proteus studied the situation, the more impossible it seemed. The root of the matter was that the sisters were simply too beautiful. Circe could not bear the sight of them. They were tall, powerful, blooming creatures, bursting with health, giving off a wild caramel musk of sea and sun. And although Circe was very handsome and stately herself, these glossy nymphs made her seem wan and haggard. She could not forgive them.

Proteus decided that the only thing he could do was separate Circe from the nymphs. He saw an opportunity to do this, for by now they had learned what he had to teach, and were ready to go into action. He called them together, and said:

"Our mistress, the goddess Athena, appeared to me last night, and gave me certain instructions which I shall now pass on to you."

"Why did she appear to you and not to me?" cried Circe. "I'll accept no instructions secondhand!"

"You'll have to take that up with Athena herself," said Proteus. "But be guided by me, dear lady, and do not provoke the goddess—not, at least, until you have practiced some magic on her behalf and showed her how valuable you can be."

"Very well," gritted Circe. "What did she have to say?"

"She recognizes that you have learned all that I have to teach about the arts of transformation, and are ready now to disrupt sea-traffic, wreck ships, and capture crews. But she wants you to divide your efforts. You, Teles and Ligiea, will be responsible for luring the ships onto the rocks, and, when the sailors have made their way to shore, you shall lead them to the palace, then return to the rocks. Circe will welcome the crews, enthrall them, transform them—and impound them in their stalls and kennels and sties. Any questions?"

"How do we get the ships to wreck themselves?" asked Ligiea.

"In a classic fashion," said Proteus. "You will go to where the rocks are thickest and most jagged, and build fires there. Such fires are the most ancient signal for clear passage and safe harborage. The helmsmen will naturally steer toward your flames, and the ships will break upon the rocks. Now to your tasks, ladies! And may the blessings of Athena attend your labors."

They dispersed. The sea nymphs went down to the shore; Circe returned to her palace to prepare her spells and potions.

What happened then made it seem as though Poseidon had somehow learned of the plot against him, and was wielding the weather to thwart it. Every night for the next month it rained, not steadily, but in sudden bursts. And these showers would fall right after the nymphs had built their fires, dousing the blaze completely, and wetting the firewood so thoroughly that it could not be used again until the next day's sun had dried it. Proteus began to grow fearful once more. He knew that without occupation the sorceress would find a way to attack the nymphs, who would surely counterattack with great enthusiasm.

He turned himself into a white seal and swam out to where the sisters perched on the rocks. He coasted onto their flat boulder and said:

"It's no use; we can't keep the fires going; we'll have to change tactics."

"Dear Proteus," said Teles, stroking his head, "we're not going to be here long enough to change any tactics."

"What do you mean?" barked the seal.

"She means we have decided to leave," said Ligiea. "We hate Circe. We love you, but we loathe her. And it's very boring here. We're going to swim back to our own waters and capsize fishing boats again. That redheaded hag can go choke herself on her potions."

"You can't go," cried Proteus. "You've pledged yourselves to the service of Athena, and must fulfill your vow, or she will avenge herself. You don't know her as I do. She's terrible when aroused."

"And we're terrible when not aroused," said Teles. "We're mouldering away here on this stupid island. Where are all the shipwrecked crews we were promised? We sit here building fires, and Poseidon rains on them, and Circe glares at us and mutters nasty things under her breath, and nothing happens, nothing at all."

"Listen to me," said Proteus. "And things will happen. We'll make them happen. That's what I came here to say. You'll no longer build these fires that only get snuffed out. You'll lure ships another way."

"What way?"

"You'll sit here on the rocks and sing—Yes! So beautifully that anyone hearing you will be enchanted and follow the sounds

"We have decided to leave," said Ligiea.
"We hate Circe. . . . And it's very boring here."

right onto the rocks. So ravishing will be your song that even if the helmsman stays on course, the sailors will dive off the decks."

"Do you really think we'll sound that good?" asked Teles. "We've always sung, but I had no idea that our voices were *that* irresistible."

"They aren't," said Proteus. "Not quite yet. But they will be. Your voices are very rich and musical—but somewhat raw.

I will train them. I will teach you to pitch your song so that it can be heard over the keening of the wind and the booming of the surf—and to fit simple words to your melodies so that they speak right to the heart."

"You can do that too?" asked Ligiea. "We know you're good at magic, but are you good at everything?"

"Not quite everything. But music is only magic that has found its voice. Trust me; I can teach you. Singing here upon these rocks, your song will be a silver noose that will catch anyone listening, that will draw them to you, and make them yours for as long as you care to keep them."

Indeed, Proteus did teach the sisters to sing. And their song was as enchanting as he had promised. Ship after ship broke upon the rocks. And when a helmsman refused to forget his duty and steered away, why then the sailors dived off the deck, as Proteus had predicted, and swam toward where the sea nymphs perched.

Teles and Ligiea, very happy with their own singing, followed the rest of Proteus's instructions. They led the sailors to the palace, where Circe then took charge. She would take her guests to a great dining hall, and serve them a bowlful of delicious red porridge, cooked according to a magic recipe. The sailors would gulp the food down greedily and immediately find themselves transformed. Whereupon the nymphs would never see the men again. Never, that is, in human form. For Circe's evil spell had changed them all into animals. Her courtyard became a zoo. Lions roamed there—wolves, elephants, wild bulls, deer, rabbits. Snakes dwelt in the grass. Trees and hedges were thronged with new birds. The kennels were full of howling dogs, the sties full of pigs; a herd of horses grazed the meadow.

Now, the nymphs, though very fond of animals, hated to see these beasts who had been men. For each of them, no matter what his shape, would gaze at the nereids with intelligent, suffering, human eyes.

Nevertheless, things went well for a while. And Athena, looking down upon the Isle of Sobs, was pleased by what she saw. She praised Proteus for serving her so well. She appeared to Circe as well, and promised that she would reward her services by making her the most powerful sorceress in all the world.

Proteus, feeling that his labors were completed, swam away from the island. He was weary of Circe and the fatal rocks and of seeing man transformed to beast. He resolved to live another kind of life for a while. So he changed himself into a bear, and, since the weather was growing cold, found a cave, and sank into a deep sleep.

Circe's evil spell had changed them all into animals.

As soon as he left the island, however, things went badly.

It happened one day that two shipwrecked crewmen quietly turned back while being led to Circe's palace, and returned to where they had come ashore. The sisters, who did not notice this, were surprised when they found sailors waiting for them upon their rock.

"You're in the wrong place!" cried Teles. "You should be with the others at the palace."

"No," said one sailor, whose name was Pero. "We're in the right place. We want to be here with you."

"You can't," said Ligiea. "It's not allowed. We'll have to take you to the palace."

"No," said the second sailor, whose name was Procles.

"Yes," said Teles. "Come on now, or we'll have to carry you."

"Please," said Pero. "Let us stay. Sit down and sing to us."

"Please," said Procles. "Do sing to us. Sing song after song. We love your voices. In fact, we love everything about you. And when you finish singing, we'll tell you stories. We've sailed to very strange places and have curious tales to tell."

As the moon climbed and paled, the sea nymphs sang their songs to the shipwrecked sailors. And, when the songs were finished, the sailors told a tale of voyages.

They had sailed to certain southern lands where the customs were different from those they had known. Trees were shaped like parasols, their fruit brown, and hairy, and as heavy as rocks. The people of this land thought that cats and monkeys were gods who had warred with more powerful gods and been shrunken into bestial shapes. But they were gods, nevertheless, and had to be worshiped.

By the time the tale was told the sailors were falling asleep. The nymphs watched them doze, and conversed in urgent whispers.

"Circe will find out," said Ligiea, "and send her servants to hunt them down. She'll go into a fit of fury when she realizes we've been hiding them. And you know what happens to anyone she takes a dislike to. She'll change these men into little animals and feed them to something big."

"What shall we do?" asked Teles.

"Look at them; they're fast asleep now. So tired, poor darlings. Circe must be asleep too. We'll take them back to the palace, right to the witching room, and do a little magic ourselves. We'll be the ones who transform them. Then they'll be able to hide themselves among the other animals. And, one day, when we find a way to get rid of the wicked Circe, we'll change the poor dear creatures back into themselves, and swim away with them."

"I suppose it's the only thing we can do," said Teles. "But it's almost dawn, so let's do it."

Tenderly, they lifted the sleeping lads from the rock, and carried them toward the palace.

All was still. Everyone was asleep. Even the dogs had stopped howling. They crossed the courtyard past the huge shadowy shapes of the animals. Earlier, a hundred eyes would have been burning holes in the darkness, but now the eyes were shuttered as the beasts twitched and moaned, clawing at the walls of a changeling dream.

Had the nymphs looked higher, however, up into the top branches of a cedar, they would have seen one pair of blazing

By the time the tale was told the sailors were falling asleep.

The sisters did not notice the owl
and had no way of realizing that
they had been observed by Circe's spy-bird.

eyes. They belonged to the owl—Athena's own special bird,
which she had given to Circe as a sleepless sentinel. The owl
watched the sea nymphs carrying the boys through the courtyard
and toward the palace gate. She spread her great wings and slid
silently into the air. By a cruel twist of fate, the sisters did not
notice the owl, and had no way of realizing that they had been
observed by Circe's spy-bird.

The nymphs entered the dark palace and made their way
to the witching room. They stretched the boys on slabs of stone
and began muttering the spells that Proteus had taught them.
Remembering the tale they had been told, they changed Procles
into a monkey, and Pero into a cat.

The monkey perched on Ligiea's shoulder. Teles had drawn
the tomcat into her lap, and was stroking him when a horrid

scream split the air, and Circe appeared before them. She was pointing a wand at them; it trembled in her hand. Her voice was so choked with rage that she could hardly utter her spell, but she managed to mumble:

> Hobble, gobble,
> I tell you that
> with these words
> You shall be birds,
> and feed the cat!

Indeed, she did intend to change the sisters into birds and feed them to the cat. But in her fury, she mishandled the powerful spell and made the mistake of beginning the transformation by giving the sisters wings. The quick-witted nereids immediately spread their new wings, flew straight at Circe, knocking her to the floor, then flew out of the room, out of the palace, off the island, and out to sea.

3

The Sirens Sing

Between the small island where Circe dwelt and the enormous island which is today known as Sicily, lay a hidden reef that could tear the bottom out of any ship that tried to sail over it. But the reef was easy to avoid because two tall flat-topped rocks stood to the northeast of it. They were a distinctive formation that could be seen for miles; when they came into view, a helmsman would simply steer to the north or to the south of the reef.

It was upon these rocks that Teles and Ligiea landed after escaping from the Isle of Sobs. They were drunk with flight, happy to have been given wings—full of glee because what had been meant as a punishment had turned into a gift. On the other hand, they felt very confused. They were changed inwardly as well as outwardly, and no longer recognized themselves. Most curious of all, they were torn by new hungers. And, in satisfying these hungers, were doing things they found repulsive.

For nereids do not eat the flesh of beast or fish or fowl. Like swans they feed upon algae and seaweed and other succulent mosses. Now, however, they found themselves as savagely rapacious as sea-hawks. On their flight they had skimmed the surface of the water, catching fish in their new talons and gobbling them raw. Flying high, they had stooped to strike birds on the wing—heron, cormorant, and albatross—and had devoured them, feathers and all.

But the sisters had been only partially transformed, and the falcon in them was warring with the loving, joyous sea-nymph nature that had once been theirs. For all that, they were too young and healthy, too intoxicated by flight to brood about themselves. There was one concern though that they could not shake off. As they grew accustomed to the wild, fear-spiced taste of raw flesh and to the warm saltiness of fresh blood, they realized that if they became hungry enough they might be tempted to make a meal of a nice plump sailor.

But thinking of sailors made them remember the two en-chanted lads they had left on the Isle of Sobs. What would become of the monkey and the cat who had been Pero and Procles? Would Circe pursue them with her vengeance? Feed them to a lion or a crocodile? Or would she forget about them and let them mingle with the rest of her zoo? If so, would they be locked in their animal shapes forever? Could they be rescued? The winged nymphs had much to wonder about as they sat on their rocks and gazed back toward Circe's island.

Out of their joy and grief and terror and wonder, they began to sing. And, hearing themselves, they realized that bird-notes had entered their voices now and made them more beautiful than ever. The heart-wrenching emptiness of the ocean waste was in their song, the seethe and chuckle of the tides, and all the shifting colors of light upon water.

They gave their song to the south wind, and it drifted out to sea. They sang and sang. The sun was sinking. Bloody light streaked the waters; the sea grew dark, then purple.

Suddenly, the sisters saw the lilac darkness bulge with a greater darkness. They heard a whipping of sails, a wrenching of wood and metal, and a clamor of men shouting. The nymphs

The heart-wrenching emptiness of the ocean waste
was in the Sirens' song, the seethe of the tides,
and all the shifting colors of light upon water.

dived off their rocks just as a ship rushed between them and broke upon the reef. The sunken rocks had torn the bottom of the ship out. It sank in a matter of minutes, dragging most of the crew with it.

A few men were struggling in the water. The sisters pulled them out and hauled them onto the rocks, where they stood, huddled and shivering.

"Sister, sister!" called Teles. "Let us not keep them. I have my reasons."

"I know," called Ligiea. "I'm growing hungry too."

"What shall we do?" cried Teles. "If we throw them back, they'll drown. They can't swim to shore."

"We'll fly them there," answered Ligiea. "But let us do it now, quickly!"

Each nymph clutched two amazed sailors in her talons, lifted them off the rock, and flew them to dry land. They set them gently on the beach and flew away as fast as they could.

The sisters returned to the rocks and sang to the moon. A new loneliness entered their song, a new amazement, and a greater hunger.

Circe's owl flew from the Isle of Sobs to the mountaintop where Athena dwelt and told the goddess all that had happened. Athena flew off and sped to the bird-women's rocks. She hovered

The sisters returned to the rocks and sang to the moon. A new loneliness entered their song.

invisibly over their perch. She listened to them sing and understood what happened to ships that sailed within reach of their voices.

All this pleased her mightily. "Ha, ha, ha," she chuckled to herself as she flew away. "Those rebellious nereids are more useful to me now than they were on Circe's island. Perched atop their rocks, singing with the voice of the sea itself, they cast their song like a silver loop about passing ships and draw them onto the reef . . . Yes! They will become a great navigational hazard, as wonderfully destructive in their own way as Circe is in hers. And every sailor that is drowned shall weaken the worship of Poseidon among seafaring people. I am pleased, very pleased with the way things have worked out. I shall give those sisters a new name: *Sirens*!"

The word meant "noose-throwers," or "those who bind." And that is the name the winged sisters were to bear till the end of time.

Afterward, however, Athena pondered the matter more deeply. "The Sirens have one weakness," she thought to herself. "They're destructive without meaning to be. They pity the shipwrecked crews, and, one day, may give way to that stupid compassion. They can't stop singing any more than a pair of nightingales can, but they may start pulling sailors out of the water—which wouldn't do at all. Now, I want to keep them where they are, singing ships onto the reef, but it behooves me to make those waters even more deadly. But how? Shall I plant a school of sharks there? No, they're very brave and strong, those nereids, and, once their pity is aroused, would not hesitate to pull a sailor out of the very jaws of a shark. I'll have to think of something worse."

She thought and thought, and finally produced a truly hideous idea.

4

Cannibal Fat

he elder gods knew that a fire as hot as the sun smouldered deep beneath the earth, sometimes burning through its crust and into the bowels of mountains, making volcanoes.

To contain this buried heat something was needed as unimaginably cold as the fire was hot. And, in the dawn of time, Uranus, the First One, accompanied by the Cyclopes and the Hundred-handed Giants, had traveled to the iciest wastes and quarried the frozen seas for what became known as "black ice"— the only substance in the universe capable of insulating the earth's surface from the fire below.

Enormous blocks of this black ice were used to construct a wall to hold the fires where they were, and to keep the surface of the earth cool enough for the seeds of life to grow. Eons later, when fish and birds and animals and man had been planted in the world, the spare blocks of black ice were kept in a cave gouged into the slope of Mount Olympus. And in this same den of abysmal frost were stored the leftover seeds and stuffs of creation.

Uranus had stationed a dragon at the mouth of the cave, for he wanted no one to enter. In time, Uranus was deposed by his own son Cronos, who then became King of the Gods, only to be deposed in turn by his own son, Zeus, who, in the family tradition, after getting rid of his father, named himself king. But under each reign, the cave remained a forbidden place, and the dragon stood eternal vigil.

Now, however, Athena needed to visit the cave to help herself to some of its taboo stores. She knew what manner of beast squatted before its portals, but the warrior goddess was not one to be dismayed by a dragon. Wearing breastplate and helmet, she carried her long spear in one hand and her shield in the other. This shield, unlike any other, was useful for more than defense; it proved deadlier than the spear. For it had belonged to the young hero Perseus—and was the one into which the image of Medusa's snake-haired head had burned itself.

In this same den of abysmal frost were stored the leftover seeds and stuffs of creation.

Athena came striding up to the cave. The dragon flailed its tail and spat fire at her. Athena lifted her shield to deflect the flames. At the same time, however, the dragon looked upon the image of Medusa and was immediately turned to stone. The goddess stepped lightly over the stone dragon and entered the cave.

She searched among sacks of seed and huge bins until she found what she wanted. It was an enormous keg, bound with hoops of copper. She broke it open; out bulged a mass of something that quivered and pulsed and glistened. She had uncovered a mass of cannibal fat, some of the primal stuff of creation, a bit of which became part of every living thing. It fed upon other forms of life and converted them to energy for its own host—whatever form that took, be it ape, dove, crocodile, or crocus.

Wielding her spear, using its sharp, leaf-shaped head as a knife, Athena sliced off a throbbing lump of blubber. She stuffed it into an empty keg, hoisted it onto her shoulder, and strode out of the cave.

On her way out, Athena knelt and breathed into the stone mouth of the dragon. The stone hide cracked, became leathery scales; the spike tail twitched; flame flickered about its maw. It was alive again, as Athena had intended. She wanted the cave to appear undisturbed so that her theft would not be discovered.

The next ship that approached the Sirens' fatal reef happened to be captained by an old, very stubborn seaman, who insisted on acting as his own helmsman, although he was quite deaf. But it was this deafness that saved his vessel. The Sirens' song didn't captivate him because he couldn't hear it, and he steered his ship clear of the reef. But his crew were young men who heard perfectly. They were noosed by the song, and jumped overboard.

The Sirens saw men swimming toward them; then they saw that the water was churning strangely. A large, glistening blob floated to the surface. They couldn't make out what it was; they had never seen anything like it before. It was a jellyfish, but huge, twenty times larger than any they had ever known. It was altogether transparent; they could see its pinkish entrails clenching.

The sailors were swimming toward it. Instead of slithering away, it moved toward them, oozing out from its own center, spreading over the surface of the water. The living aspic covered the men, curled about them, folding over on itself. And the

Out bulged a mass of something
that quivered and pulsed. . . . She
had uncovered a mass of cannibal fat.

horrified nymphs saw that the men were inside the creature, completely wrapped in glistening jelly.

The Sirens tried to scream but couldn't interrupt their song. They kept singing as they watched the men being digested.

The sisters had no way of knowing that it was Athena who had dropped that primal lump of cannibal fat into the sea, where it became, quite naturally, a carnivorous jellyfish. What they did know was that it meant certain death for any sailor to fling himself overboard in those waters—knew that their song was a death-song now, made more deadly by its very beauty. Nevertheless, they couldn't stop singing any more than the wind can stop blowing or brave men can turn back from danger.

5

The Meadow Nymphs

Before bees began, there was a clan of meadow nymphs who had learned to plunder flowers of their sweetness and to distill the fragrant juice with the cider of apple, fig, and pomegranate, making a drink so magically delicious that anyone who tasted it wanted nothing else.

One day when the nymphs were brewing their potion in a big pot, the odor floated to the top of Olympus where the gods dwelt. Down swooped Zeus and Hermes to see what smelled so good. They smiled with pleasure when they saw the cluster of meadow nymphs, for the leaf-clad creatures were very fresh and lovely. Two nymphs drifted toward them, bearing dripping ladles, and crying "Taste! Taste!"

Zeus gulped down a ladleful of the drink. He drank again, then raised his arm and spoke:

"O lovely creatures of meadow and field, I thank you for concocting this marvelous potion. But you must control your overflowing generosity, my dears. For all sweetness carries a sting, and those tasting this drink will find their idea of themselves foolishly enlarged. They may fancy themselves immortal—a condition reserved, as you know, for me and my family. Therefore, to avoid trouble, this drink, fit for the gods, is hereby declared fit *only* for the gods. All lesser breeds shall be forbidden to drink it. Is this understood?"

"Yes . . . yes . . ." murmured the nymphs, pressing about him. They never really listened to what any male of any species had to say—god, demigod, or mortal—but they were expert at reading face and gesture, and knew that Zeus was feeling very pleased and important. So they pretended to understand what he had said, and queued up for his blessing—which he bestowed heartily upon each, with a hug and a kiss, Hermes assisting.

Whereupon, the gods flew off believing that they had passed a solemn law, and the nymphs drifted to their flowerbed, giving no thought at all to what had been decreed.

So it was that the drink became known as *nectar*, or "deathless", and was not only the favorite beverage of the gods but the foundation of their diet. Boiled with ground yellow wheat kernels, it was used as a food, and was known as *ambrosia*, or "immortality". And the gods feasted daily upon nectar and ambrosia.

It happened one day that a nymph running across the meadow found her way blocked by a flock of sheep. Without pausing, she leaped onto the back of a ram and, stepping lightly from sheep to sheep, raced over the tightly packed mass. Then she heard a curious mewing sound. She leaped down and ran to a ewe that was sprawled on the grass somewhat separated from the others. Kneeling, the nymph saw that the ewe was suckling a human infant, a boy.

Looking about, she saw bloody rags on the grass, a bloody tuft of wool, some raw bones—and realized that the child's parents must have been eaten by wolves, and that the baby had found his way to a mother sheep whose newborn lamb had also been eaten. The nymph cradled the infant in her arms and raced back to her sisters who shouted with joy when they saw the beautiful babe. They immediately adopted him, vowing to care for him

Down swooped Zeus and Hermes to see what smelled so good.

as no child had ever been cared for. Indeed, they raised the child tenderly and merrily, and he was very happy among them. But Cora, the nymph who had found him in the field, was always his favorite, and she doted on him. *Butes* was the name he was given, meaning "herdsman."

He grew into a boy, golden-skinned, lithe as a satyr, with a poll of reddish-brown hair and amber eyes that could turn almost yellow. The nymphs swore that those eyes glowed in the dark—like a cat's.

The beautiful boy grew into a beautiful youth, and was the cause of the first quarrels among the clan. For every nymph in the meadow planned to marry him as soon as he was ready. Now, this was the only flaw in the boy's happiness. Butes loved them all, and couldn't bear the thought of disappointing any one of

43

them. Actually, he felt quite ready to select a mate—but was trying to put off the day of decision by pretending to be more childish than he felt.

Nymphs are not easily fooled in such matters, though, and things were growing tense. One of the larger ones lost her patience one evening, slung Butes over her shoulder, and began to run off into the woods with him. But she was caught by Cora, who broke a branch over the head of the abductress, and snatched him back.

Then she took him aside, and said: "My child, you are a child no longer."

"Of course not!" he cried. "I'm grown up—or almost."

"Yes," she said. "You're almost a young man—almost ripe. And my sisters of the glade are growing restless, very restless. Each of them wants you for her own, and they are accustomed to going after what they want."

"Dear Cora," said Butes. "Please understand that I have done nothing to encourage them."

"They don't need much encouragement," said the nymph. "One look at you is enough. And spring is almost upon us. The moon kneels lower each night, and shines more hotly. I can't keep knocking them over the head one by one, as they try to carry you off."

"What can I do about it? Go away?"

"Just for a little while," said Cora. "Just to give them time to roam meadow, grove, and stream for shepherds or woodsmen or satyrs—enough for all."

"I don't mind going," said Butes. "I'm getting restless too. Perhaps I'll go to sea."

"To sea?"

"Sometimes I walk on the beach and watch the ships spreading their wings to the wind, and I want to be aboard."

"No, no!" cried Cora. "Sea voyages are too long. And too perilous. There are storms, shipwrecks, monsters—all sorts of dreadful things can happen."

"You know, I think I'd like danger. I've never even seen a monster."

"If I have my way, you won't," said Cora. "But you can see something even more exciting. As you know, twice a year we of the Meadow Clan deliver our nectar to the gods. We take turns making the journey to Olympus. My idea is for you to make the next trip. It will take you away from here for a month or so. Give you a chance to visit the gods in their own wonderful home, and perhaps make some useful contacts. A friend or two in high places do a young man no harm. By the time you come back, each nymph will be paired off, and you will be safe for another year—by which time, perhaps, you will have chosen someone for yourself."

"That can only be you, dearest Cora."

"We'll see." she murmured, kissing him in a way that meant she had already seen all she had to. "But go, my child," she whispered. "You must not linger. By first light, we shall begin loading the donkeys, and off you shall go."

Indeed, the nymphs began to load the donkeys at daybreak, and had finished before the sun was high enough to dry the grass.

*"If you are to live long enough to
be my mate," said Cora, "you shall
need the special protection of a god."*

Butes, wrapped in a cloak against the morning chill, kissed each
nymph goodbye, saving Cora till last. She drew him aside, and
gave him a crystal flask.

"What's this?" he asked.

"Something you'll need," she said. "I had a dream last
night, the kind that shines a light into the darkness of time to
come, showing us more than we want to know. Monstrous perils

are to be flung into your path, my lovely boy. If you are to live long enough to be my mate, you shall need the special protection of a god."

"Which one?"

"You shall meet them all on Olympus, and be able to choose for yourself. When you select one, be it fierce Ares, subtle Hermes, radiant Apollo, or deft Hephaestus, give him this crystal flask, making sure no one else sees you do it."

"What's in it?"

"Nectar. Ordinary nectar. But you shall describe it as something extraordinary—drawn from a blossom hitherto unknown and of matchless flavor, and especially brewed by the clan-mother herself for the exclusive use of whichever god you offer it to."

"But," said Butes, "when he tastes it, won't he know it's the same nectar he's been drinking every day?"

"No," said Cora. "He'll believe what you have told him. It is a god's nature to welcome praise and to magnify it even as he hears it. He'll swallow every word of your tale about the special nectar in the flask. Vanity will combine with imagination to convince him that your gift is all you say it is. And he will stand ready to befriend you—at least until someone else gives him a better gift."

"I shall do as you bid, dearest Cora. But must it be a god? How about a goddess?"

"No!" cried Cora. "Not a goddess! Any goddess you give that to will immediately boast about it to the other goddesses to make them jealous—and she'll succeed. You'll have gained one goddess as a friend, and the rest as enemies."

"You are as wise as you are beautiful," said Butes. "I'll do exactly as you say."

"The sun is climbing fast. You must be off."

"Farewell," said Butes. "I shall return."

6

A Fatal Gift

When Butes led his string of donkeys through the marble pillars that marked the entrance to the garden of the gods, he was met by a hundred-handed giant named Briareus who served Zeus as doorman and porter. The giant swiftly unloaded the donkeys, and holding a heavy keg of nectar in each pair of hands—there were fifty kegs—he carried them easily up the garden path toward the palace.

Butes understood that his beasts could not be allowed to enter the garden because they would eat the flowers. He led them a short distance downhill, then turned them out to pasture on the slope.

The peaks of the Olympian range wear snow in the winter, but the dwelling of the gods is divinely shielded from the weather. In palace and garden it is always June.

Dusk had fallen by the time Butes had climbed the slope again. The gods were preparing to dine. Their table stood in the garden. It was a massive slab of marble resting on four tree stumps. This evening, the younger gods were dining alone, for their elders had been summoned to High Council by Zeus, and were meeting in his throne room.

Dusk had fallen by the time Butes had climbed
the slope. . . . The gods were preparing to dine.

The hundred-handed Briareus had a brother equally well-furnished with hands, who was the gardener for the gods. His name was Botanus, and he had traveled the world over seeking the most exquisite flowers to transplant upon Olympus. He had also hunted down those songbirds whose voices were sweetest and brought two of each to nest in the trees around the palace. At dusk in that garden the voices of the birds thronged the air, and the scent of the flowers hung most heavily. Music and fragrance became one, a distillate of that happiness which is the natural element of the gods—who, walking in their garden at dusk, were reaffirmed in their divinity, and worked up an appetite for dinner.

Butes passed between the marble pillars and into the garden where the gods had begun to dine. The lad dared not approach. He clutched the flask of nectar and stood there, gawking.

The gods were clad in light. Apollo in golden light, shot with crimson. His sister Artemis in pearly shifting hues, hot silver fading to silver-brown, turning to sunken fires as when the moon

50

hangs over the sea, watching itself drown. Ares was cloaked in the ominous smoulder of watch-fires, the tragic glare of funeral pyres. Hephaestus was lit by the bright open flame of the forge. Hermes was clad in a strange, blue-silver light, as of cold intellectual fires. Athena brooded in owl-light, the murderous dusk in which the great bird hunts.

Bewildered by radiance, diminished by awe, Butes fell to his knees before the glorious assemblage. He wanted to sink lower than his knees, roll in adoration before them like a dog rolling in the dust. As he knelt there, a fragrance reached him. The fragrance became music, the music of a voice speaking just to him, murmuring, "Butes, arise!"

He arose, feeling himself fill with powerful joy. At the end of the great table he saw another light—a soft light, but one that seemed to swallow all the rest. A soft pink flame as of roses filtering sunlight, becoming fragrance, turning to birdsong. He saw the rosy light parting, as when a beautiful woman brushes away a plume of hair that veils her face.

There, at the end of the table, was the naked face of beauty itself—the face of Aphrodite, Goddess of Love.

Forgetting all that Cora had warned him against, he leaped onto the table. Threading his way through flagons and platters and past the astounded faces of the feasting gods, he raced toward Aphrodite. Kneeling before her, he thrust the flask at her with both hands, crying:

"For you, Aphrodite! For you alone!"

By the last glimmer of twilight, Aphrodite led Butes through the garden. She was murmuring to him, but he couldn't answer. He was choked with joy. She wore a blue tunic, and her feet were bare. A dove rode her shoulder. She led Butes to the roses. The rose was her flower as the dove was her bird. Among trees, the apple was sacred to her, and the myrtle.

"I value your gift," she said. "And I value him who brings it even more. But you have been rash."

"Because the other goddesses will be jealous?" asked the lad.

"Yes, sweet boy."

"I would risk more than their wrath to please you, my lady."

"Nevertheless," said Aphrodite, "their anger is to be feared. When you leave this place, I want you to take certain precautions. Do not go hunting. For Artemis is the Huntress Maiden, Queen of the Chase; she can turn an arrow or spear in mid-flight. And some hunter, trying to aim at a deer or a wild boar, will find himself accidentally killing you."

"I shall shun the chase," said Butes. "I don't like to kill animals anyway."

"Do not walk across ploughed fields," said Aphrodite. "They are ruled by Demeter, who may send a snake to bite your heel."

"I shall avoid ploughed fields," said Butes.

"To fend off Athena's wrath is more difficult," said Aphrodite. "She is implacable when seeking vengeance. I shall have to buy her mercy. She covets a certain marvelous mirror made for me by my husband, Hephaestus; it permits me to see the back of my head when combing my hair. I don't know what good it will do her; she's always wearing that ugly helmet—but she wants it anyway. I'll give her the thing if she agrees to forgive you."

"Your beauty is matched only by your kindness to me, O Queen of the Night."

"We may fail to appease their wrath, no matter what we do," said Aphrodite. "So I shall try to protect you with my most potent charm. By rose and by dove, by apple and myrtle, I enjoin that no harm shall come to you for what you have done today. In the name of love and beauty and brave, foolish enraptured generosity, let all hear this:

Butes, Butes,
I give you power
over bird and flower.
Things with wings
shall attend you,
and night and morn,
the watchful thorn
defend you.

She took him in her arms
and kissed his face. "Now leave
this place," she said. "As swiftly
and silently as you can. Collect
your donkeys and hurry home to
your meadow. And be very care-
ful along the way."

But the other goddesses
were waiting beyond the garden
wall, and even Aphrodite had
not gauged the depths of their
jealousy.

"Remember the early
days?" said Artemis. "When we
used to thin out the swarming
mortal herd by a great all-night

*"By rose and by dove, by apple and myrtle, I
enjoin that no harm shall come to you for
what you have done today."*

hunt with dogs and horses and torch-bearers? There's nothing
I'd rather do tonight. Anyone else in the mood?"

"Why, I can't think of anything I'd enjoy more!" cried
Athena.

"That ill-mannered little wretch seems to move quite
spryly," said Artemis. "He should give us a good run."

"I'm definitely in the mood," said Athena.

"So am I," said Demeter.

"It seems a bit cruel," said gentle Hestia. "But our dogs do
need the exercise, don't they, Artemis? So it would be a kindness
to them, wouldn't it?"

But the other goddesses were waiting
beyond the garden wall, and even Aphrodite
had not gauged the depths of their jealousy.

"We'll give him a sporting chance," said Artemis. "Allow him a big headstart and course him in the forest instead of the open field, so that he'll be able to dodge around and hide behind trees and so forth. It'll be a great chase."

"How will we get him away from Aphrodite?" asked Demeter.

"She won't keep him in the garden long," said Artemis. "He's too small for her. Besides, I happen to know that she'll be otherwise engaged this evening."

"Oh? . . . With whom?" asked Demeter.

"Apollo, Ares, Hermes . . . anyone *but* her husband. Now I'm off to fetch my hounds."

"I'll go call the torch-bearers," said Hestia.

"I'll round up the horses," said Athena.

"I'll stay here and see that he doesn't slip away," said Demeter.

The goddesses separated. The gods were still at the table. It was a hunter's moon, almost full, bright enough to cast shadows.

7

Manhunt

All night long, Butes had been running for his life. Now at dawn, he was still fleeing, pursued by the hounds, and torch-bearers, and screeching goddesses. By daybreak, the pack had flushed him out of the woods and into an open field. He could run like a hare, but he was weary now, and the dogs were gaining fast. Mingled with their baying was the thunder of hooves and the bloodthirsty screams of the goddesses, riding close behind the hounds.

"This is it," thought Butes. "I'm about to die. Pity . . . it's too beautiful a morning for such sad things to happen. Not that I'd go gladly even if the weather were foul. But my options seem to have run out. Let me try to persuade myself in these final moments that a kiss from Aphrodite is worth a painful death. So I'll take a last look at that kindling sky, and try to be thankful. Last looks are too late, but what can I do?"

He fixed his eyes on a strange opalescent cloud that was floating above his head. He didn't know that he was looking at the underside of dove wings—those of Aphrodite's messenger pigeons, whose colors changed with every changing light. They were not there by chance. Aphrodite had dispatched them on an urgent errand. Each one carried a rose-branch in its beak.

The dogs' howling turned to snarls as they came in for the kill. Their glittering eyes and savagely grinning muzzles were very close now. Behind them Butes saw weapons gleaming: the spear of Athena, poised for throwing; the silver arrow that Artemis was notching; Demeter's sharp pruning knife.

Things were dropping between him and the dogs. Butes cringed away; he thought the goddesses had begun to throw their weapons. What pierced the ground, however, were not weapons, but rose-branches dropped by the pigeons. They were planting themselves, as Aphrodite had instructed. Magically empowered by the blessing of the love goddess, the rose branches dug themselves into the earth, and a wall of thorns began to grow. A thick impenetrable hedge of barbed branches wove themselves about the crouching boy.

The springing hounds found themselves impaled on the thorns. They tore free, and fled, whimpering. The goddesses reined back their horses and rode around and around the hedge. Artemis shot her silver arrows into it. Athena flung her spear. But neither could pierce the densely woven thicket. Cursing, Athena scooped up her spear and flung it again. It stuck harmlessly in the tangled branches.

"Let's burn it down!" cried Demeter. "I'll command the torch-bearers to relight their torches."

"Those branches are too green to burn," said Hestia.

"Not if the fire is hot enough," said Athena.

"Besides," said Demeter, "even if they only smoulder, the smoke will suffocate him."

Then, to the astounded goddesses, it seemed as if their very words had summoned fire. A zigzag bolt of blue lightning sheared the air. Thunder spoke out of the clear sky. The thunder became the voice of Zeus, and that voice was full of fury.

Aphrodite, after dispatching her doves and her roses to protect Butes, had flown to the King of the Gods, and cried:

*It seemed to Butes like the most
beautiful morning he had ever known.*

"Your daughters and your sisters defy you, Zeus! At this very moment they are disobeying your edict against man-kill. Bearing a grudge against a poor lad, they are hunting him to his death. Look down, look down! Behold how your subjects disport themselves as your benign attention is occupied with mighty matters of state. Behold!"

Zeus, who always found it difficult to resist Aphrodite, looked down and saw that she spoke the truth. He was enraged,

and made himself even more majestic in his fury because Aphrodite was watching, and he wanted her to admire him. So he flung his lightning bolt and spoke in a voice of thunder, frightening the four goddesses out of their wits, causing them to turn their steeds and scatter in every direction.

Aphrodite seized the great knotted hand of Zeus and kissed it. She smiled her most radiant smile, one that told him her gratitude knew no limits. Then she raised her arm, and the thorn-hedge fell away from Butes.

The field was empty. The sun had climbed now. Birds rejoiced. It seemed to Butes like the most beautiful morning he had ever known. And life— every breath and throb and leaf whisper and birdnote—seemed infinitely precious.

"Thank you, Aphrodite," he murmured. "And my thanks to you, O thundering Zeus. The nectar my nymphs shall make

Cora and her party were among the flowers, but each could see the others darkening, dwindling . . .

60

for you will be sweeter than ever. And twice as often now, shall we bear our brimming kegs to your mountain home."

But Butes was never to see his nymphs again. For Athena, festering with hatred, leaped off her horse and whistled up her owl-chariot. The great white arctic owls—larger than eagles—drew the chariot swiftly through the sky until they were over the meadow where the nymphs dwelt.

Cora and her party were among the flowers, plundering them of their sweetness. The chariot dipped. Athena pointed her hands and mumbled a curse the way a snake shoots venom through its hollow teeth.

To the nymphs below it was as if the summer afternoon had become a hot golden fist. They were gripped so tightly that they couldn't move their heads to look down at themselves. But each could see the others darkening, dwindling, sprouting hair upon their bodies—saw many-paned eyes bulging, membranous wings growing. By the time Athena drove off, cackling triumphantly, the entire clan of lovely meadow nymphs had become a swarm of bees.

They tried to speak to each other, tried to call to Zeus and Hermes who had once praised them. They pled with the gods to annul the curse, to restore them to themselves. But instead of their own voices, they heard only the sound of buzzing and realized that their prayers would not be answered, and that they would never be permitted to return to their own shapes.

Of all things in the world, love clings most stubbornly to old forms, and Cora so passionately wanted to be recognized by Butes when he returned that she was partially shielded from Athena's curse. Though transformed into a bee like the others, she had become their queen, and for an hour each day was granted speech.

*The entire clan of lovely meadow
nymphs had become a swarm of bees.*

And it was Cora who told Butes what had happened when
he returned to the meadow and found the nymphs gone, replaced
by a swarm of strange creatures among the flowers. He tried to
choke back his tears, tried not to show how horrified he was at
the sight of the fat black and yellow bee that hovered at his ear,
whispering.

"Do not grieve, my boy. But look to your own safety. For the ruthless Athena hates you still. You must leave this place, go as far as you can, as swiftly as you can."

"No," he cried. "When I leave here I shall go to Aphrodite and beg her to restore you. She saved me from the wrath of Athena; perhaps she'll do the same for you."

"No, no," cried Cora. "You must not go to her. I am enchanted now, even though the enchantment be foul, and am able to see the future. If you return to Olympus, you are doomed. What you must do is go to sea. You wanted to do that once—remember? Well, now you must. For Poseidon, Lord of the Sea, is Athena's enemy and may protect you against her."

She darted off suddenly and vanished among the flowers.

Butes, blinded by tears, stumbled out of the meadow and headed for the beach.

"There's nothing for me here," he murmured to himself. "If there's anything for me anywhere, perhaps I'll find it at sea."

8

Butes

thena appeared to Circe on the Isle of Sobs and said: "A ship sails this way. On board is a youth whom I loathe beyond anyone else in the world. His name is Butes."

"Well, my lady," said Circe. "If he lands here, you'll soon be rid of him."

"Listen carefully," said Athena. "I want you to bestialize the crew, but not Butes."

"He is to be spared?"

"Certainly not. I don't want him alive in any shape or form. I'm lending you my owl-chariot. You'll be able to fly over the ship and drop a spell upon the crew, turning them into a pack of starving wolves. But allow Butes to retain his own form. He won't keep it long. The wolves will tear him to pieces."

"All shall be done according to your wish," said Circe. She climbed into the owl-chariot and flew off.

The chariot streaked across the sky until Circe spotted a ship below. The owls flew lower, and the sorceress studied the deck to see if she could identify Butes, whom Athena had described.

But she herself was being identified by two pairs of very sharp eyes. She had come near enough to the reef for the Sirens to recognize their enemy. Their song changed, rang with trumpet notes, became a battle hymn, as they rose off the rock and flew toward the chariot.

Their wings were powerful. High above the owl-chariot they arced—then dived, screaming. The owls saw what seemed like eagles diving upon them, talons poised. Like terrified horses kicking a coach to pieces, the owls frantically pecked themselves free from the traces and flew away as fast as they could.

The chariot, of course, plunged toward the sea. Circe barely had time to turn into a bat and slip out before Athena's chariot hit the water and sank.

Circe had done well to become a bat for it flies faster than any bird, and the one thing she wanted now was to escape the Sirens. She sped homeward and was so frightened, and so unused to being frightened, that she remained a bat for hours before returning to her own form.

The Sirens flew back to their rock and began to sing their triumph. But their joy turned to astounded grief when they saw the ship they thought they had saved rushing toward them. The wind was gusting. "Pray that they're blown away from the rocks," whispered Teles.

Just as she spoke, the vessel was caught in a crosswind. Its sails flapped. The ship yawed, but before it could be blown away from the reef, sailors began jumping overboard and swimming toward the magical song.

The Sirens kept singing and their voices filled with grief as they saw the enormous slime spreading toward the swimmers.

The ship was heading straight toward them. A slender lad had lashed himself to the great sweep-oar, and was guiding the ship upon the reef. Again the wind shifted, growing into a gale, hurling the vessel toward the line of sunken boulders. It hurtled between the Sirens' rocks. As it passed, the helmsman swung a knife, cutting himself free of the steering oar, and leaped off the deck.

As he fell, Ligiea, still singing, rose into the air and caught him in her arms. She set him down gently on the rock. Teles flew over and joined them.

*Again the wind shifted, growing into a gale, hurling
the vessel toward the line of sunken boulders.*

Butes lay sprawled between the bird-women, breathing
their salt fragrance, and wrapping himself in the sound of their
wonderful voices. As he listened he began to feel alive for the
first time since losing Cora. Felt himself fill with a wild
inventiveness.

"One of you, take me in your claws!" he said. "Fly over
that vile aspic monster, and hover there; I want to watch him at
work."

"Why?" said Ligiea, as Teles kept humming. You'll only
see him digesting your shipmates. It's not a pleasant sight."

"To vanquish an enemy," said Butes, "you must get very
close. It's rarely pleasant but always necessary. Will you take me
there, please?"

Teles kept singing as Ligiea grasped the boy in her talons,

spread her wings, and flew off the rock. She flew over the jellyfish, and hovered there, dangling Butes from her claws.

He studied the huge blob as it fed upon his shipmates. He gritted his teeth, fought down nausea, and forced himself to watch. Forced himself to examine every bit of the monster, and watch every movement it made.

While it seemed shapeless at first sight, he recognized that it had a definite physique, although blurred. The center of the creature was slightly sunken, and seemed softer than the edges. That hollow served as mouth and gullet. The edges of the blob gripped its prey and folded it toward the middle, where the mouth sucked it down toward pink intestines.

The jellyfish had swallowed itself completely—all but its mouth, which became a brief whirlpool . . . then vanished.

"I have a plan," he yelled to Ligiea over the wind. "But it's dangerous. May I ask you to share the risk with me?"

"You *are* asking," answered the Siren.

"If my plan works, it will rid your waters of this horror."

"What must I do?" asked Ligiea.

"Hold me by the ankles. Circle away and come flying back, dipping low enough so that my hand may just skim the surface."

Hearing the steely ring of the lad's voice, seeing the set of his jaw and the frosty gleam of his eye, she asked no further questions, but shifted her grip so that she held both ankles in one set of talons. Then she circled in the air, and flew back, dipping low, so that his hand just brushed the water.

That hand held a curved scaling knife. And when Ligiea flew over the jellyfish which was devouring the last of the sailors, Butes stabbed his hand down, and hooked his knife into the edge of the blob.

Ligiea felt a great weight dragging her. She beat her wings with all her strength. The edge of the jellyfish, impaled by the knife, began to fold over onto itself—toward its own center. Butes pulled as hard as he could, helping the Siren drag the ruffled edge of the monster into its mouth.

That mouth went into its blind senseless suck, drawing the edge of itself into its own intestines. Butes managed to pull his arm away just in time, and Ligiea flew off with the lad dangling from her claws.

Tighter and tighter curled the jellyfish as it gorged upon itself. It became one long scroll of slime, growing narrower and narrower until it had swallowed itself completely—all but its mouth, which became a brief whirlpool, a spool of bubbles, then vanished.

Butes nestled on the rock between the two Sirens. "Now," he said, "sing to me. I'm the only one here who can listen, and be safe, listening. Sing me to sleep, and do not wake me until I've finished my dream."

9

A Taste of Nectar

By this time, changeable Proteus had decided to change sides again. He left Athena's service and re-entered the employ of Poseidon. The sea god, who was very experienced in the ways of the world, viewed treachery as a natural form of self-interest, and was willing to accept Proteus's vows of renewed loyalty.

"Your first assignment," said Poseidon, "is to do something for the young man who's being so tormented by Athena. That vicious shrew turned the nymph he loved into some kind of sticky stinging bug. See if you can change her back. I'd like to do a good turn for so brave a lad. Besides, the quality of the nectar has fallen off terribly. The stuff we're being served on Olympus now doesn't compare to what we were getting before Athena cursed the nymphs."

Proteus swam off and returned shortly thereafter. "It's no use, master," he said to Poseidon. "Athena used a specially adhesive curse. I've tried my most powerful spells and still can't restore the bee to nymphhood."

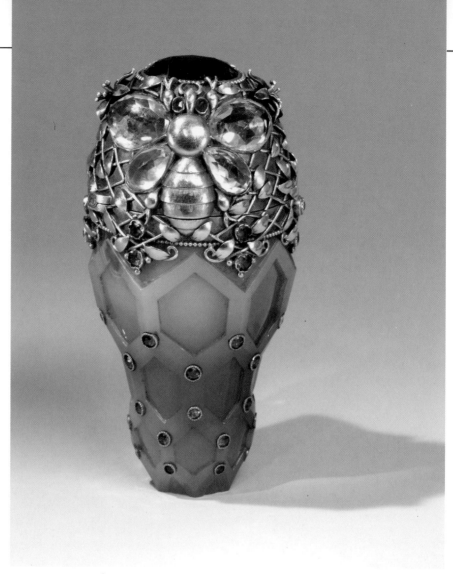

When told that Cora could never
be a nymph again, Butes had asked to
be transformed into a bee himself.

"Well, think of something," said Poseidon. "The nectar's getting worse and worse. I think those stupid bees have been nibbling garlic. I'll have to stop dining at Olympus unless things improve."

Proteus swam away again and found Butes on the Sirens' isle. The bird-women were cooing over him gently. Proteus returned to Poseidon's cave and told the sea god that he had consulted with the youth—who, when told that Cora could never be a nymph again, had asked to be transformed into a bee himself.

"I obliged him," said Proteus. "I changed him into a handsome young drone, and he flew off to join the swarm."

Some weeks later, a beaming Poseidon informed Proteus that the quality of the nectar was indeed improved.

Ulysses and the Sirens

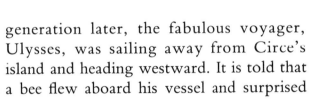 generation later, the fabulous voyager, Ulysses, was sailing away from Circe's island and heading westward. It is told that a bee flew aboard his vessel and surprised Ulysses by addressing him in fluent Greek.

"Disregard my appearance and heed my words, O captain," said the bee. "I was once a man like you, hunted by the gods over land and sea. Having long admired your career, I wish to help you now."

"What makes you think I need help?" asked Ulysses.

"Having escaped Circe's vile enchantments, you are now headed toward an even greater peril. Ignore my words and be shipwrecked, watch your crew drown, and be drowned yourself. But accept this gift and use it well, and you may be able to save yourselves."

"What gift?"

"This ball of wax. It is pure beeswax, drawn out of the finest combs in all the world."

"And how can this ball of wax do all the wonderful things you have promised?"

"Very soon," said the bee, "if you keep on this course, you will hear the sound of singing, borne by the wind. That sound is utter enchantment, irresistible. Whoever hears it must follow it. But if you follow it, if you steer your ship toward where the Sirens sing, you will hit a hidden reef that will tear your ship apart. Nor is there any use trying to steer clear, for when your men hear the song they will dive overboard and swim to their destruction. The Sirens' rock is white with the bones of sailors."

"You seem to know what you're about," said Ulysses. "Speak on."

Butes told him what to do, and flew away. Whereupon, Ulysses called his crew together and issued his commands. They grumbled, but no one on this ship ever disobeyed their captain.

Knowing this, Ulysses told the men to listen well for he was about to give them unusual instructions. "You must obey me," he said, "until I am bound to the mast. Then, no matter what I do, no matter what signals I make for you to release me, you must ignore them, and keep me tied to the mast. For I shall have lost my senses, and shall be issuing crazed commands."

He took the ball of wax that the bee had given him, broke off bits of it, and stuffed the ears of each man so that he could hear nothing but the pounding of his own blood. Then, as they had been instructed, two of the men bound Ulysses to the mast— bound him very tightly. For Ulysses did not dare deafen himself. In those days, sailing the high seas in such small ships, a captain had to hear the changing sounds of wind and sea, or he would endanger ship and crew.

The sailors finished lashing Ulysses to the mast just in time. For now he heard the sound of singing. The song was faint at first and Ulysses was able to keep his wits about him sufficiently to signal the men to drop the sail and unship the long oars. For the wind was off the reef now, and the small square sail of the vessel would not have allowed it to skirt the deadly reef.

The men could not hear the Sirens' song, and bent strongly to their oars. But Ulysses heard the voices clearly now, and wished he had plugged his own ears with wax. Every drop of his blood surged toward the sound of those voices. Every pore

*The men could not hear the Sirens' song, and
bent strongly to their oars. But Ulysses heard.*

and muscle ached with the song—yearned to reach it. He felt his
hair trying to pull itself out of his head, felt his eyeballs trying
to fly out of their sockets. Bound to the mast, it seemed to him
that the sun was charring him where he stood—that he could
actually *see* the Sirens' voices, pouring in a crystal flood through
the burning air.

Ulysses moaned and yelled and gibbered but the crew,
obeying his orders, ignored him. The voices formed a silver noose
that fell about his neck and began to pull at him. He knew that
he would have to break loose from the mast or choke to death.
His mighty muscles swelled. He burst the rawhide bonds and
dashed toward the edge of the deck.

But two of his strongest men were standing guard, as he
had instructed. They seized him before he could dive overboard.
He struck them down, but they had stopped him long enough
to give the crew time to leap out of their rowing seats, and seize
him.

They crushed him under their weight, then dragged him back to the mast, and bound him with the huge hawser that was the anchor-line. Again, Ulysses strained at his bonds, howling to be released. He knew he could not break the hawser, but he was trying nevertheless to force himself upward from bended legs, using all his furious strength to uproot the mast, rip it out of its hole.

The men heard the wood of the mast groaning under the strain. But it held. Ulysses could not uproot it. One of the sailors who had held Ulysses, however, had lost the wax out of his ears and been knocked to the deck unconscious. Now, as he came to, he heard the Sirens singing. He rushed to the rail and dived overboard.

Ulysses saw the sharp triangular fin of a shark cutting the water toward the swimmer—heard the man scream, saw him

We can still hear the Sirens sometimes when we're out on the water.

sink in a bloody froth. The other men, their ears still plugged, kept rowing.

The voices grew fainter and fainter, and finally died away. Ulysses felt the madness ebb slowly out of his body. He signalled to his men to unplug their ears and unbind him.

The captain stood at the stern, looking back toward the Sirens. They were too far away now. All he saw was what looked like two enormous birds in the distance.

Thousands of years have passed since then. But the Sirens have not quite gone. When the gods declared themselves immortal, what they meant was that nothing in nature really dies; it only changes form.

So it is that we can still hear the Sirens sometimes when we're out on the water—not in a motorboat, but in a sailboat or some other craft that slips silently through the chop. At times, we can hear the wind change pitch, bearing the sound of women singing.

We may hear them, but we do not see them. Nor do their voices linger long on the air. For they are smothered by the din of motorboats, rumbling barges, steam-whistles, helicopters, and low-flying airplanes.

"Sister, sister, take heart," one whispers to the other. "Those who swarm so noisily must soon drive themselves off the earth. Their foul vapors will blow away, the waters will clear. A pure primal hush will fall again upon the sea—and we Sirens shall be heard once more. We shall again raise our voices to mingle with the wind, sending a crystal coolness to those who thirst for adventure."

Acknowledgments

Letter Cap Illustrations by Hrana L. Janto

Opposite page 1, ATHENA FLYING HER OWL, *Greek statuette (ca. 5th century B.C.), bronze (H. 5 15/16")*
  Courtesy of The Metropolitan Museum of Art, New York, Harris Brisbane Dick Fund, 1950 (50.11.1)

Page 2, TWILIGHT, *by Pierre Bonnard (1867-1947), oil on canvas*
  Courtesy of Private Collection, Winterthur
    Photo: Giraudon/Art Resource, New York

Page 5, SEAL, *by Gaston Lachaise (1882–1935), bronze statuette (11 x 14½")*
  Courtesy of the Whitney Museum of American Art, New York (Acq. #31.43)

Page 8, BULL, *sculptural relief from Knossos Palace, Crete (ca. 1500 B.C.)*
  Courtesy of Heraclion Museum, Crete
    Photo: Jan Lukas/Art Resource, New York

Page 9, TIGER *by Edward J. Detmold, color etching (13¾ x 7⅞")*
  Courtesy of The Metropolitan Museum of Art, New York. The Elisha Whittelsey Collection, The Elisha Whittelsey Fund, 1967 (67.809.16)

Page 10, BLUES (1962) *by Adolph Gottlieb, oil on canvas*
  Courtesy of The National Collection of Fine Arts, Washington, D.C.
    Photo: Art Resource, New York

Page 12, NEPTUNE I (1985/87), *by Earl Staley, acrylic on canvas (62½ x 47")*
  Courtesy of the Texas Gallery, Houston

Page 13, STORM AT SEA *by Pieter Brueghel (1525(?)–1569), oil on canvas*
  Courtesy of Kunsthistorisches Museum, Vienna
    Photo: Kavaler/Art Resource, New York

Page 14, GOLDFISH *by Gustav Klimt (1862–1918), oil on canvas*
  Courtesy of Giraudon/Art Resource, New York

Page 16, PASSING SONG *by Albert Pinkham Ryder (1847–1917), oil on canvas (22 x 11 cm.)*
  Courtesy of the National Museum of American Art, Washington, D.C.
    Photo: Art Resource, New York

Page 18, THE ENCHANTRESS CIRCE *by Dosso Dossi (ca. 1480–1542), oil on canvas*
Courtesy of Galleria Borghese, Rome
Photo: Scala/Art Resource, New York

Page 21, A SEA NYMPH *by Emile Vernon (19th century), oil painting*
Courtesy of Christie's, London
Photo: Bridgeman Art Library/Art Resource, New York

Page 23, CIRCE AND HER LOVERS IN A LANDSCAPE *(ca. 1525) by Dosso Dossi, oil on canvas*
Courtesy of the National Gallery of Art, Washington, D.C., Samuel Kress Collection
Photo: Art Resource, New York

Page 25, HEAD OF MAN WITH CLOSED EYES *by Francesco Vanni (1565–1610), black and red chalk drawing (14⅜ x 9⅞")*
Courtesy of The Metropolitan Museum of Art, New York, Gift of Cornelius Vanderbilt, 1880 (80.3.163)

Page 26, NIGHT OWL *(1975) designed by James Houston, glass (7½ x 7¾"), limited edition of thirty*
Courtesy of Steuben Glass, New York

Page 28, THE STORM SPIRITS *by Evelyn De Morgan (1855–1919), oil on canvas*
Courtesy of De Morgan Foundation, London
Photo: Bridgeman Art Library/Art Resource, New York

Page 31, THE SLAVE SHIP *by J. M. W. Turner (1775–1851), oil on canvas*
Courtesy of the Museum of Fine Arts, Boston
Photo: The Bettmann Archive, New York

Page 32, MOONLIGHT, WOOD'S ISLAND LIGHT *by Winslow Homer (1836–1910), oil on canvas (30¾ x 40¼")*
Courtesy of The Metropolitan Museum of Art, New York, Gift of George A. Hearn in memory of Arthur Hoppock Hearn, 1911 (11.116.2)

Page 34, AND OUT OF THE CAVES . . . *by Hans Hofman 1880–1966, oil on canvas (84⅛ x 60¼")*
Courtesy of the University Art Museum, University of California, Berkeley; Gift of the Artist (1965.4)

Page 36, UNTITLED *by Jackson Pollock (1912–1956)*
Courtesy of Sipa-Press/Art Resource, New York

Page 38, UNTITLED *by Joan Miro (1893–1983)*
Courtesy of Ray Wilson/Art Resource, New York

Page 40, PANDORA *by Bertrand Jean (called Odilon) Redon (1840–1916), oil on canvas (56½ x 24½")*
Courtesy of The Metropolitan Museum of Art, New York, Bequest of Alexander M. Bing, 1959 (60.19.1)

Page 43, MERCURY AND JUPITER "VIRTUS" *by Dosso Dossi, oil on canvas*
Courtesy of Kunsthistorisches Museum, Vienna
Photo: Saskia/Art Resource, New York

Page 44, THE GOOD SHEPHERD, *marble statue (ca. 5th–6th century)*
Courtesy of the Vatican, Museo Pio Cristiano
Photo: Scala/Art Resource, New York

Page 46, FLORA *by Carlo Gignani (ca. 17th century), oil on canvas*
Courtesy of Galleria Estense, Modena
Photo: Scala/Art Resource, New York

Page 48, BACCHUS *by Cornelis van Haarlem (1562–1638), oil on canvas*
Courtesy of Boymans Museum, Rotterdam
Photo: Kavaler/Art Resource, New York

Page 50, OLYMPUS *by A. Appiani (1754–1817), oil on canvas*
Courtesy of Pinacoteca, Brera
Photo: Scala/Art Resource, New York

Page 53, THE TOILET OF VENUS *by Francois Boucher (1703–1770), oil on canvas (42⅝ x 33½")*
Courtesy of The Metropolitan Museum of Art, New York, Bequest of William K. Vanderbilt, 1920 (20.155.9)

Page 54, HUNT OF DIANA *by Domenichino (1581–1641), oil on canvas*
Courtesy of Borghese Gallery, Rome
Photo: Scala/Art Resource, New York

Page 56, DIANA *by Augustus Saint-Gaudens (1848–1907), gilded bronze (H./reduction 28¼")*
Courtesy of The Metropolitan Museum of Art, Gift of Lincoln Kirstein, 1985 (1985.353)

Page 59, GARDEN AT VERNONET *by Pierre Bonnard, oil on canvas*
Courtesy of Musee, Bagnols-Sur-Ceze
Photo: Art Resource, New York

Page 60, WOMAN AND FLOWERS *by Odilon Redon (1840–1916), oil on canvas*
Courtesy of Beveler Gallery, Basel
Photo: Scala/Art Resource, New York

Page 62, DETAIL FROM THE BALDACCHINO *(the transept of St. Peters) by Bernini (1598–1680)*
Courtesy of the Vatican
Photo: Saskia/Art Resource, New York

Page 64, HALF–FIGURE OF A YOUTH WITH HIS RIGHT ARM RAISED, *drawing by Simone Cantarini (1612–1648), red chalk, a few white highlights, on beige paper (33.8 x 26.7 cm.)*
Courtesy of The Metropolitan Museum of Art, New York, Rogers Fund, 1969 (69.1)

Page 67, FLYING DUTCHMAN *(ca. 1887) by Albert Pinkham Ryder, oil on canvas*
Courtesy of the National Collection of Fine Arts, Washington, D.C.
Photo: Art Resource, New York

Page 68, THE WHIRLPOOL *by Kupka, 20th century, oil on canvas*
Courtesy of Beaux-Arts, Grenoble
Photo: Scala/Art Resource, New York

Page 70, GLORIFICATION OF THE REIGN OF URBAN VIII, *ceiling fresco by Pietro da Cortana (1596–1669)*
Courtesy of Palazzo Barberini, Rome
Photo: Scala/Art Resource, New York

Page 72, PERFUME CONTAINER *(ca. 1893) made by Tiffany & Co. for the Columbian Exposition, gold and semi-precious stones (H. 3⅝ D. 1¾")*
Courtesy of The Metropolitan Museum of Art, New York, Gift of the Duchess de Mouchy, 1965 (65.143)

Page 74, NYMPHS OF THE STARS *by Sir Edward Burne-Jones (1833–1898), gouache and gold*
   Courtesy of the National Museum of Wales, Cardiff
      Photo: Bridgeman/Art Resource, New York

Page 77, ULYSSES AND THE SIRENS *by Herbert Draper (1864–1920), oil on canvas*
   Courtesy of Ferens Art Gallery, Hull
      Photo: Bridgeman/Art Resource, New York

Page 78, THE SEA AT SUNSET AT DIEPPE *by Eugène Delacroix (1798–1863), oil on canvas*
   Courtesy of the Louvre, Paris
      Photo: Scala/Art Resource, New York

BOOKS BY BERNARD EVSLIN

Merchants of Venus
Heroes, Gods and Monsters of the Greek Myths
Greeks Bearing Gifts: The Epics of Achilles and Ulysses
The Dolphin Rider
Gods, Demigods and Demons
The Green Hero
Heraclea
Signs & Wonders: Tales of the Old Testament
Hercules
Jason and the Argonauts